Sea Life Scientist

Have You Got What It Takes to Be a Marine Biologist?

by Lisa Thompson

Compass Point Books ✦ Minneapolis, Minnesota

First American edition published in 2008 by
Compass Point Books
3109 West 50th Street, #115
Minneapolis, MN 55410

Editor: Robert McConnell
Designer: Lori Bye
Creative Director: Keith Griffin
Editorial Director: Nick Healy
Managing Editor: Catherine Neitge
Content Adviser: Steven Haddock, Ph.D., Bioluminescence
  and Zooplankton, Monterey Bay Aquarium Research Institute,
  Moss Landing, Calif.

Editor's note: To best explain careers to readers, the author has
created composite characters based on extensive interviews and research.

 This book was manufactured with paper containing
at least 10 percent post-consumer waste.
Printed in the United States of America.

Library of Congress Cataloging-in-Publication Data
Thompson, Lisa, 1969–
  Sea life scientist : have you got what it takes to be a marine biologist? / by Lisa
    Thompson.
      p. cm.—(On the job)
  Includes index.
  ISBN 978-0-7565-3620-6 (library binding)
  1. Marine biologists—Vocational guidance—Juvenile literature. I. Title. II. Series.
  QH91.45.T46 2008
  578.77023—dc22   2007035558

Image Credits: Brand X Pictures, cover (all); NOAA Geophysical Fluid Dynamics
Laboratory, 39; SeaWorld, 45 (top). All other images are from one of the following
royalty-free sources: Big Stock Photo, Dreamstime, Istock, Photo Objects, Photos.
com, and Shutterstock. Every effort has been made to contact copyright holders of
any material reproduced in this book. Any omission will be rectified in subsequent
printings if notice is given to the publishers.

Visit Compass Point Books on the Internet at *www.compasspointbooks.com*
or e-mail your request to *custserv@compasspointbooks.com*

Table of Contents

A Marine Biologist on the Job   4

Why Are Coral Reefs So Important?   6

The Four Big Threats to Coral Reefs   8

Global Warming and Coral Reefs   10

What Does a Marine Biologist Do?   12

How I Became a Marine Biologist   14

All in a Day's Work   18

Who's Who on My Team?   20

What a Marine Biologist Studies   22

Humans Helping Corals, Corals Helping Humans   24

Equipment Checklist   26

The Trip!   28

Back on Land   36

What Our Trip Showed   40

Losing Nemo   42

A Checklist and Job Opportunities   44

Find Out More   46

Glossary   47

Index   48

A Marine Biologist on the Job

Finally all is ready for our trip to the reef. It's going to be a busy four days. The weather looks as if it will be great. Things are always hectic just before a research trip. There's lots of checking and rechecking of equipment and lists.

Tomorrow I am leading a team of marine biologists who will spend four days looking at the current state of a section of coral reef. The area we are going to is just off the coast of Australia, in the Great Barrier Reef.

Moon jelly

Coral reefs are like underwater cities for sea creatures!

A turtle glides by overhead.

Lion fish

The Great Barrier Reef is an extensive coral reef system that stretches more than 1,240 miles along the northeast coast of Australia. It is the largest structure on the planet built entirely by living organisms.

The Great Barrier Reef is made up of about 2,900 separate reefs. The coral reef boasts a diversity of species rivaled in number only by the diversity found in tropical rain forests.

Why Are Coral Reefs So Important?

Coral reefs are home to many unique animals and plants that could not survive anywhere else. Tens of thousands of plant and animal species live in coral reef areas.

Coral is very important in controlling how much carbon dioxide is in the oceans. Without coral, the amount of carbon dioxide in the water would rise dramatically, which would affect all living things on Earth.

Coral reefs also protect coastlines from strong currents and waves by slowing the water down before it reaches the shore. That's why they are called barrier reefs.

On this trip we, as marine biologists, want to see how the reef community is surviving. There has never been a research dive done in this area. We want to see whether the reef is being threatened in any way.

Today the main threats facing coral reef communities are coral disease, coral bleaching, the crown-of-thorns starfish, and humans. We hope the information we gather will help find better ways to manage and conserve this reef and others around the world.

PUN FUN Seagulls that fly over the bay are called bay-gulls!

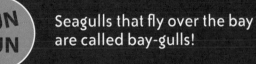

The huge number of species of animals and plants on the Great Barrier Reef includes:

- At least 360 species of hard corals, including 10 found nowhere else, and one-third of all the soft corals in the world
- Six of the world's seven species of marine turtles
- At least 200 bird species
- At least 30 species of marine mammals, such as whales and dolphins
- At least 500 species of seaweed or marine algae
- At least 1,500 fish species
- At least 5,000 species of mollusks, such as snails

The Four Big Threats to Coral Reefs

Coral diseases

Scientists believe that runoff nutrients and sediment from the land, as well as high sea temperatures in summer, can cause coral diseases. There are about 30 known coral diseases, and the Great Barrier Reef has at least six of them. They include black-band disease, white syndrome, and coral tumors. Coral diseases are carried and spread by bacteria, fungi, algae, and worms.

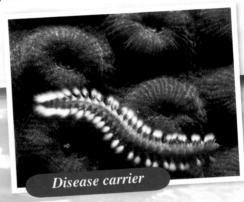

Disease carrier

Coral bleaching

Increasing sea temperatures cause corals to lose their color, go white, and eventually die. Reef corals are very sensitive to sea temperatures. A rise of just one degree of average water temperature over the summer is enough to cause coral bleaching in many species. Some corals can recover if the sea cools. However, coral that has been bleached is generally weaker and is also more prone to attack from disease.

Bleached coral

Crown-of-thorns starfish

Small numbers of this starfish on a reef are normal. They are simply part of the coral reef ecosystem. In large numbers, they eat corals faster than corals can grow and reproduce. A crown-of-thorns starfish eats an area of coral the same size as itself in a single day. In one year, one animal can destroy 6 square yards of coral. If there are hundreds of them on a reef, it means destruction of the reef.

Coral muncher

Humanity

People damage coral reefs in three main ways—through pollution, tourism, and fishing.

Not all coral reefs around the world are as healthy as the Great Barrier Reef. Since 2000, almost 30 percent of the world's reefs have been destroyed. It is estimated that 11 percent have been lost because of humans, through pollution, overfishing, dynamite fishing, mining of sand, or onshore building and development. Scientists think two of every three reefs could disappear in the next 40 years. We need to protect and preserve these rain forests of the sea.

Effects of pollution

Global Warming and Coral Reefs

The world is getting warmer. Coral bleaching occurred in almost all tropical oceans as far back as 1997. Reef areas in the Maldives, Sri Lanka, Kenya, Tanzania, and the Seychelles have been greatly affected by bleaching.

In 2002, the worst bleaching ever recorded occurred in the Great Barrier Reef. It affected 60 percent of surveyed reefs, and the damage was very severe in some areas. Most reefs survived, but full recovery of badly damaged reefs may take decades.

Reef types

There are three kinds of coral reefs: fringing reefs, barrier reefs, and atolls.

- **Fringing reefs** grow right up to the shore.

- **Barrier reefs** are separated from the shore by a wide, deep lagoon.

- **Atolls** are coral reefs that surround a shallow lagoon. They are created when an island that is surrounded by barrier reefs sinks below the water, leaving a circular reef, the atoll.

Top views

Side views

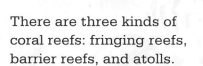

Fringing reef

water
coral
land

Barrier reef

coral
land

Atoll

coral
coral
land

Biologists wonder: Why so many starfish?

Why do crown-of-thorns starfish numbers get out of hand? No one knows the answer yet, but one theory is that the runoff from chemicals that are used in farming is allowing more starfish eggs to survive.

Another reason could be that the main predator of the crown-of-thorns starfish is the giant triton (a large sea snail), and the triton has been hunted extensively by people. The giant triton's shell is a popular souvenir.

Damaged coral that has washed up on the beach

PUN FUN   Marine biologists like to see a friend or sea anemone.

What Does a Marine Biologist Do?

It's the job of a marine biologist to study living things in the sea. Traveling to exotic locations on research trips is only one small part of what we do.

A large part of the work of a marine biologist is done away from the water. A marine biologist conducts research and experiments to find answers to specific questions about sea life, the ocean, and its surrounding environment.

From the vast oceans to the smallest tidal pool, the sea holds many amazing things to discover, study, and understand.

Coral Reef Regions of the World

- Indo-Pacific
- Western Atlantic
- Red Sea

How I Became a Marine Biologist

To become a marine biologist takes more than a college degree and a flair for science. You also need a passion for ocean life. It's a lifestyle you really do "submerge" yourself in.

I've always loved the ocean. When I was 6, my dad took me snorkeling for the first time while we were on vacation. I couldn't believe how amazing everything was—the sea grasses, the fish, the animals that lived on and under the rocks, the corals. I was hooked! Under the surface of the water was a completely weird and wonderful world, and I wanted to know as much about it as I could. I started keeping records of all the strange things I saw. Then I collected as much information about them as I could find.

Growing up, I snorkeled whenever I got the chance. I was very interested in how fish lived, so I had a tank in my bedroom filled with various species of fish.

Checking out sea life

14

Seahorses are among the slowest fish in the world. At top speed, some species take two and a half days to travel two-thirds of a mile. Seahorses are very unusual because it is the male that becomes pregnant.

Sea cucumbers breathe through their bottoms! They can also vomit a mass of sticky white threads to confuse and trap their enemies.

Manta rays use electro-receptors to locate their prey. They use the small flaps located beside their mouths to help them capture plankton.

Parrotfish sleep in their own sleeping bag. From their mouths, they secrete mucus that covers their body. The mucus protects them from predators while they are sleeping.

As I got older, I learned to surf and dive. This let me enjoy the ocean even more. At school I really liked science subjects. When it came time to go to college, there was only one thing I wanted to become—a marine biologist. It took four years of hard study in science until I finally got my degree.

Marine biology is a profession with many specialized branches. The area I chose to specialize in is called marine ecology. Marine ecology is the study of the relationships between marine plants and animals and their environments.

Learning to dive was fun!

During and after my time in college, I spent many weekends and holidays volunteering my skills for environmental organizations. Finding full-time work as a marine biologist was difficult, since it is a very competitive field with few openings. Volunteering was a good way to gain experience and show my dedication. One of my volunteering stints was with the research team I work for now. That's how I became one of their marine biologists.

Surf's up!

Subjects to study and certificates you will need

High school courses:
Math—for all those statistics
English—to write and present reports (join the debating team for practice)
Biology—the foundation of it all
Chemistry—this will help the biology make sense
Physics—a huge advantage
Computers—makes data processing easier

College courses:
Marine science or biology
Botany
Ecology
Fish biology
Molecular biology
Marine mammalogy
Physiology
Conservation courses

Certificates:
Scuba-diving certificate
Boat license

There's a lot of life in there!

All in a Day's Work

A typical day for a marine biologist can include many things:

- Checking specimen tanks
- Doing maintenance on research and experimental equipment
- Preparing food for the lab animals and feeding them
- Collecting samples
- Attending meetings
- Doing research
- Writing research reports
- Giving lectures about what research has shown

Skilled hands required

There are many specialized areas of marine biology, but in all of the areas you need to:

- Collect, analyze, and organize information
- Communicate ideas and write findings
- Plan and organize
- Work with others in a team as well as work alone to pursue answers
- Use technology

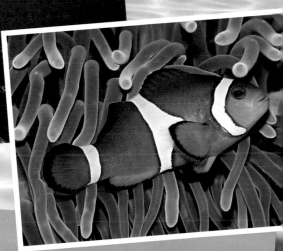

Undersea symbiosis

The word *symbiosis* comes from "sym," which means together, and "biosis," which means life. Symbiosis happens when two organisms create a union from which each benefits.

Certain fish, such as clownfish, are immune to the sting of the sea anemone. They take shelter in the anemone's tentacles. Some fish, such as the juvenile rough scad, even swim within the tentacles of sea jellyfish. They act as bait, so the sea jelly can sting and trap other fish. In return, the fish get to share the meal with the sea jelly.

Who's Who on My Team?

My team is an organization made up of marine biologists, each with special knowledge in a particular branch of marine biology. The type of research required on a field trip determines who is on the team.

On this particular trip, apart from me and Tom, who is the skipper of our research vessel and a qualified research diver, there are four other team members.

Everyone has his or her own role to play in gathering the information and collecting the data. We need to get a complete "big picture" of what life is like on the reef so we can study and analyze it when we get back on land.

Me Because I am the team leader in this expedition, my job is to make sure we collect information in all areas, to give us the best scientific "big picture'" of the reef. As a marine ecologist, I will be keeping a special eye on how all the living things that rely on each other are surviving as a community.

William is a marine zoologist. Marine zoology is the study of the animals that live in the sea. William's special interest is marine invertebrates. Invertebrates are animals that do not have backbones, such as sea worms, sea slugs, sea stars, lobsters, and sea jellyfish. William is going to be keeping count of the number of invertebrate animals that call this reef home.

Allison is a marine botanist. She is a specialist who studies ocean plants. Allison will be collecting samples of sea grasses and algae. The reef is home to about 500 species of seaweed or algae. Most seaweeds are types of algae, and they provide an important food source and breeding ground for many reef animals. Allison is also going to look at zooxanthellae (zoe-zan-thell-ee)—the single-celled algae that live within coral and help build reefs.

Dan studies coral. He is an expert coral research scientist. Dan will be looking at the types of coral on the reef, the amount of dead coral compared with live coral, and the age of the coral. He will also be recording the amount of limestone on the reef. Over time, dead coral becomes limestone, and this will give us a good idea of how old this part of the reef is.

Emily is also a marine zoologist. She has a special interest in ichthyology (ick-the-all-uh-gee)—the study of fish. Emily will study the fish populations and the variety and biodiversity of fish on the reef. Biodiversity is the number of species in an area.

What a Marine Biologist Studies

Marine biologists do a lot of things. Here are some of the specialized branches of marine biology:

Marine mammalogy is the study of mammals that live in the ocean, a category that includes whales, manatees, and dolphins.

Ichthyology is the study of fish.

Parasitology is the study of marine parasites.

Marine bacteriology is the study of bacteria that live in the sea.

Marine biochemistry is the study of chemicals in marine plants and animals.

Marine physiology is the study of how marine plants and animals breathe, grow, and move.

What is coral?

Coral looks like a plant, but it is really an animal related to the sea jellyfish, often with a few plant cells added. The plant part means that corals can use energy from the sun to make their own energy. They can photosynthesize, which means they can convert sunlight into simple sugars. Photosynthesis is something only plants can do.

In the process of photosynthesis, sea plants release oxygen into the water. Much of the world's oxygen, which humans and animals need to breathe, is produced by this process. The rest is produced through photosynthesis by trees, shrubs, grasses, and other plants.

Humans Helping Corals, Corals Helping Humans

Marine biologists may have found a new form of first aid for injured coral reefs. Researchers at the University of Guam have managed to grow 10 species of coral. They hope this will lead to the "farming" of coral by aquarium suppliers. Live patches of farmed coral could be applied to reefs that have been damaged, helping the reefs to regenerate. Someday there even could be a bank of corals to be transplanted into damaged reefs all over the world.

Corals help humans in many ways, and some of those ways are personal. Corals, for example, can be used to make medicines. Australian scientists have developed a sunscreen from substances found in coral. The corals use the substances to protect themselves from the sun's ultraviolet light. It has an SPF (sun protection factor) of more than 50. Even animals that live in the coral help humans. Scientists in the United States have created a potent pain-killing drug from the poison of reef-dwelling sea snails.

Green button polyps

Mushroom coral

Coral comes in all kinds of colors.

Types of Coral

There are more than 500 species of coral. They have a wide range of shapes, sizes, and colors, yet they all have the same basic body plan—a simple sacklike stomach and a mouth that is surrounded by a ring of poison-filled tentacles.

A single part of a coral is called a polyp. Each coral polyp makes a limestone cup around itself and spends the rest of its life inside, only sticking out its tentacle at night to feed. A coral colony is about a million of these individual polyp shells, all stuck one on top of the other. When coral polyps die, new ones grow right on top of the old, empty skeletons.

Brain coral

Staghorn coral

Bubble coral

Equipment Checklist

Here's a list of some of the specialized equipment we will be taking on this trip:

✓ **diving gear**
wet suits, fins, masks, air tanks, regulators, weight belts

✓ **collecting bags**
When a sample is collected, it has to be marked with specific information, like the dive date, location, time, and temperature of the water, and then put in its own bag.

✓ **portable GPS (global positioning system)**
This lets you know your exact location.

✓ **manta board**
A diver using a manta board is towed under water behind a small boat. This lets the diver survey a large area in a short time. There is very little water movement, so the animals on the reef are not scared away. The boat stops every two minutes so the diver can record data.

✓ **microscopes**

✓ **thermometers**

✓ **nets**
to collect plankton and fish samples

✓ **collecting buckets**

✓ **specimen jars**
a variety of sizes: small, medium, and large

✓ **underwater camera**

✓ **underwater video cameras**

✓ **slates and pencils**
to write under water

✓ **measuring tape**
to mark transects, which are areas to be surveyed and recorded

✓ **bottom corers**
to sample seabed sediment

Pure or applied?

There are two kinds of scientific research:
- Pure research, which seeks new knowledge in a certain area
- Applied research, which tries to solve real-life problems

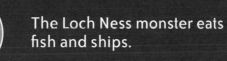

PUN FUN

The Loch Ness monster eats fish and ships.

The Trip!

August

Day 1

We head out early. The sea is calm. The team and I again go over the important things we would like to do on this trip and how we will achieve them. We reach our destination by 10 A.M.

Anchors up!

We mark out a field area—the area of the reef where we will concentrate our study. The sun is shining and the water is crystal clear. We get to work immediately. Allison, William, Dan, and I go in for a dive to do a visual survey of the area. I take the video camera to record our first impressions. Visibility is excellent. It feels great to be back in the water.

Starfish and coral on a reef

Allison gathers samples of seaweed. She places the samples in separate collecting bags, making sure to mark the date, site location, time, tide, and temperature of the water.

Emily conducts a visual fish count. With William's help, she marks out a square transect area and begins counting. She notes the number of small fish compared with the number of large fish, so she can see how they are breeding. She also counts the number of fish species, so she can get an idea of the fish biodiversity of the reef.

Emily notices that the parrotfish have been feeding on some brain coral. Parrotfish have unusual mouths with large teeth that are fused together like a beak. They use their beaks to bite off tiny pieces of stony coral (the size of fine sand) to eat.

Check out the teeth on this parrotfish!

PROJECTS

INFORMATION

FINANCIAL

ADDRESSES

29

August

A large sea turtle swims by and happily lets me capture it on video. In the

Look at this beauty!

afternoon, Dan and I take the underwater cameras into the water. We take photos for the coral visual library we are compiling back at the lab. William takes the first of many water samples to be tested. Measuring water quality is one way we can see whether humans have affected the reef and, if so, how much.

Day 2

Dan and Allison carry out an extensive survey of the types of coral found in the area. Dan compares the number of hard corals and soft corals. Emily takes more water samples. She also uses a plankton net to scoop up samples. By measuring the plankton's abundance, Emily can begin to estimate the size of the fish population.

Sponge

First link in the chain

Phytoplankton are the basic food of all ocean life and the foundation of the marine food chain.

Some plankton can only be seen under a microscope. They are tiny organisms that float freely and drift with the ocean currents. Plankton is made up of tiny plants called phytoplankton and animals called zooplankton.

Zooplankton feed on other plankton. They include single-celled organisms, crustaceans like krill, and even the larvae (babies) of mollusks, squid, lobsters, and sea stars.

Plankton—so tiny, but so important

Emily looks at four types of nutrients found in the water—nitrate, nitrite, phosphate, and silica. These nutrients, along with sunlight, are needed by phytoplankton for growth and survival. Healthy phytoplankton nutrient levels mean lots of healthful food for the reef.

Emily also checks the water for signs of pollution and chemicals from farming and urban development or from passing ships. Clear, high-quality water is vital for a healthy reef. Reefs can only grow in sunny, shallow, and clear water.

William does an invertebrate count. Sample sea slugs and sea worms are caught to be taken back to the lab. William's experiments will give us a better understanding of invertebrates and their role in the reef community.

Headed for the oceans

The amazing Christmas tree worms

Nudibranchs are colorful sea slugs, but they taste awful.

Day 3

Today Dan, William, and Allison take the smaller boat so Dan can do a crown-of-thorns starfish count using the manta board. William and Allison stop the boat every two minutes so Dan, who is looking around under water, can survey the area and record his numbers on a slate board.

Being towed with a manta board—cool, eh?

August

After the broad-overview survey is done, they come back to join me. Dan, William, and I dive together to do a fine-scale survey. We divide the area into 40 transects (covering an area 165 feet long by about 17 feet wide) and count all the crown-of-thorns starfish we see in a transect. We also record their size, to give us an idea of how old the starfish are.

The crown-of-thorns starfish eats coral.

It's just so huge!

The manta board survey lets us estimate how many adult starfish are in a wide area of the reef. The fine-scale survey lets us see exactly how many starfish are in our field area. The fine-scale survey gives us a more accurate number, while the manta board survey gives us an estimate of the number in the surrounding area.

We use compare-and-contrast techniques with all our research results. We compare the results with others from similar areas and with past results from this reef. This gives us a bigger picture of what is going on here and now, what's normal, and how things have changed.

Samples from the ocean floor

Day 4

Since this is our last day, everyone is busy getting the last samples to take back to the lab and doing final species counts.

Samples of the reef floor are taken using the bottom corer.

All the samples are checked to see whether they are marked correctly. The water in the fish tanks is changed so that all the living samples stay healthy.

We all take final dives. I do a final video survey of the reef while Allison takes photos with the camera. Around noon, Tom, the skipper, lets us know there is a change in the weather approaching. When the sea becomes choppy, we pack up and leave the reef at about 2 P.M.

A sea dragon, up close

35

Back on Land

Now the hard work begins. We must study and run tests on the many samples we collected out in the field. After that, we will begin to compile, analyze, and organize our research.

When scientists put together their research findings, they must look at the work with an open mind. It is important not to be biased by what you feel, but instead to draw your conclusions from the evidence.

Working carefully with samples

Observation in the wet lab

Our research center has two types of laboratories—dry and wet. The dry lab is filled with basic scientific equipment like microscopes and computers to conduct experiments and record findings. There is also video and camera-imaging equipment and an array of specialized machines to carry out advanced testing.

The wet lab has all kinds of tanks and refrigerators for holding samples and conducting experiments. It also has a tank that houses a living reef. Thousands of gallons of seawater are continuously circulating through the tank's filters. The room the lab is in is temperature-controlled and light-controlled.

This is where we bring our live coral fish, plant samples, and invertebrates. We monitor their life cycles, feeding habits, and other details in the controlled environment of the wet lab.

The science lab where we carry out our research

Studying the results

A month after our return, we are still gathering the results of our research on the trip. Some of the experiments are continuing, but the information gathered so far is enough for each team member to present his or her findings.

Emily found that fish numbers were strong and there was a healthy biodiversity of fish on the reef. Plankton levels were good for maintaining such fish populations. This reef is part of an area in the Great Barrier Reef where fishing is banned. Fish numbers in areas closer to the coast where fishing is still allowed show less diversity and only a third of the fish numbers found on this reef.

Keeping up fish numbers depends on having protected areas.

Coral colonies affected by rapid temperature change

Can reef-building corals adapt to these rapid climate changes?

NOAA GFDL CM2.1 Climate Model

-20 -16 -13 -11 -9 -7 -5 -3.6 -2.8 -2 -1.2 -0.4 0.4 1.2 2 2.8 3.6 5 7 9 11 13 16 20 °F

Surface Air Temperature Change [°F]

(2050s average minus 1971-2000 average)   SRES A1B scenario

What Our Trip Showed

Dan found that the coral, in general, was very healthy. Further tests showed that water quality was excellent for coral growth to continue.

A significant number of crown-of-thorns starfish was recorded in the field area, but not enough to cause major damage. We will continue to monitor their numbers.

Allison found there was a wide range of plant life. She discovered some very interesting results about the nutrition and chemistry of some algae species. Her research into these topics is ongoing.

William found more than 15 types of invertebrates in the field area. The sea worms he brought back from the dive have settled in well and are thriving in the wet-lab reef. He is still conducting experiments on their feeding habits.

How healthy coral should look

Overall, we found this area of the reef to be in good to excellent condition. There was little or no evidence of coral bleaching, coral disease, or crown-of-thorns starfish damage. Human impact on this section of the reef has been minimal. To make sure this situation continues, the area has been included in an ongoing yearly monitoring program.

Once our research has been compiled and organized, it will be time to put it into documents, tables, and graphs and present it, so others can see the results. Marine biologists spend a lot of time writing about their research findings, both to let others know what they have found and to apply for grants to support further research.

Losing Nemo

The film *Finding Nemo* made clownfish so famous that suddenly many people wanted them in their fish tanks at home. They are now at risk of extinction in ocean waters around Thailand because of the great demand for them as pets.

Some fish hunters even resort to using poisonous chemicals that make all the fish in the water pass out and float to the surface. The desired fish are then plucked from the top of the water. Many of the fish left in the ocean never recover from the poison.

PUN FUN

The group of singers wore coral necklaces.

To cope with the situation, a breeding program was started in 2000 in an attempt to save the real Nemos and increase their numbers. The program has been successful in breeding seven species of anemone fish (clownfish) found in the Andaman Sea and the Gulf of Thailand.

Some of these fish are sold directly to fish stores. Others are released into the ocean, but only on the condition that people living in the area protect the fish from poachers, who want to sell them.

Scientists plan to breed other kinds of aquarium fish that people like to own but are on the brink of extinction.

A Checklist and Job Opportunities

Before you decide to become a marine biologist, ask yourself some questions:

1. Will you finish your high school courses, getting good grades in math, English, biology, and chemistry?

2. Will you get a bachelor of science degree in college, taking courses in subjects like marine or environmental biology or aquaculture? You may even go further and earn a master's degree or Ph.D. in a relevant field.

3. Have you considered that marine biologists often work on short-term contracts and move around a lot? Remember that biologists rarely work with large sea mammals like whales or dolphins—usually zoologists do that. You're more likely to work with the small end of the food chain—bacteria, plankton, and algae.

4. Are you curious about life in the sea?

5. Would you rather do something you enjoy than something that will pay you a lot of money?

If your answer to these questions is yes, you may have a successful future in studying sea life.

Fish conservation

An unusual chance to work with a large mammal

Where do marine biologists work?

Marine biologists work in a variety of fields:

- Conducting fish studies and ocean-protection research for governments and conservation organizations
- Researching marine life for private companies to develop cures for diseases
- Lecturing and teaching in schools and colleges
- Saving animals and doing research for marine parks
- Researching and creating exhibits for museums
- Writing, consulting, and researching for government environmental agencies, the news media, and filmmakers

Advising filmmakers

PUN FUN If you see a whale, it could be a fluke.

Find Out More

In the Know

- The employment of biological scientists, a job category that includes marine biologists, is expected to grow at about the same rate as other occupations.

- Job opportunities for marine biologists will continue to be limited because the field is small.

- Marine biologists often concentrate on molecular biology, the study of biochemical and genetic processes inside living cells.

- Scientists who study fresh-water organisms are called limnologists.

- The average yearly pay for the category of biological scientists that includes marine biologists is about $63,500. The lowest 10 percent in this category (which includes most beginning scientists) earn $34,300 or less. The highest 10 percent earn about $95,000 or more.

Further Reading

O'Neill, Michael Patrick. *Fishy Friends: A Journey Through the Coral Kingdom*. Palm Beach Gardens, Fla.: Batfish Books, 2003.

Ward, Nathalie. *Do Whales Ever . . . ?* Camden, Maine: Down East Books, 1997.

Williams, Andy. *Nature Unfolds Oceans*. New York: Crabtree Publishing Co., 2002.

Woodward, John. *Tidal Zone*. Chicago: Heinemann Library, 2004.

On the Web

For more information on this topic, use FactHound.

1. Go to *www.facthound.com*
2. Type in this book ID: 0756536200
3. Click on the *Fetch It* button.

Glossary

algae—photosynthesizing organisms found in or near water, ranging from single cells to giant kelp

biodiversity—biological diversity in an environment, as shown by numbers of species of plants and animals

biologist—scientist who studies living things

botanist—scientist who studies plants

carbon dioxide—natural gas, produced by animals breathing, that is absorbed by plants

crustacean—marine invertebrate with a soft, segmented body and a hard, segmented shell, with pairs of jointed legs

data—information gained from studying something

ecologist—scientist who studies the relationships between organisms and their environments

ecosystem—community of organisms interacting with each other and their environment

GPS—global positioning system; a satellite navigational system that is used to calculate position

invertebrate—animal without a backbone

krill—shrimplike ocean crustaceans that live in large swarms

mammalogy—branch of zoology that studies mammals

mollusk—marine invertebrate with a soft, unsegmented body enclosed in a hard shell

nutrients—beneficial substances taken in or eaten by living things

organism—any individual living animal or plant

plankton—plants and animals that drift in the ocean; they form the start of most marine food chains

polyp—tiny, columnlike animal that makes up coral

regulator—scuba-diving device that controls and changes air pressure

sediment—materials such as sand, gravel, and clay carried along by water; dregs that settle at the bottom of a liquid

transect—part of an area to be scientifically studied

zoologist—scientist who studies animals

Index

algae, 40, 44

animals, 5, 6, 7, 9, 15, 18, 19, 21, 23, 29, 30, 31, 37, 42–43

atolls, 10

barrier reefs, 4–5, 8, 9, 10, 28–30, 32–35, 38, 40–41

biodiversity, 21, 29, 38

character traits, 14, 36

clownfish, 19, 42–43

co-workers, 4, 18, 20–21, 28, 29, 30, 32, 33, 34, 38

conservation, 7, 9

coral, 23, 25, 29, 30, 40

coral bleaching, 7, 8, 10, 40, 41

coral diseases, 7, 8, 41

coral farming, 24

coral reefs, 4–5, 6–7, 8, 9, 10, 12–13, 21, 28–30, 32–35, 38, 40–41

coral research scientists, 21

crown-of-thorns starfish, 7, 9, 11, 33–34, 40, 41

diseases, 7, 8, 41

education, 14, 16, 17, 44

equipment, 4, 18, 26, 37

Finding Nemo (film), 42

fringing reefs, 10

giant tritons, 11

Great Barrier Reef, 4–5, 8, 9, 10, 28–30, 32–35, 38, 40–41

humans, 7, 9, 41

ichthyology, 21, 22

invertebrates, 21, 32, 40

job description, 4, 12, 18, 28–30, 32–35, 36–37, 41

job opportunities, 45

laboratories, 37, 40

manta boards, 33, 34

manta rays, 15

marine bacteriologists, 22

marine biochemists, 22

marine botanists, 21

marine ecologists, 16, 20

marine mammalogists, 22

marine physiologists, 22

marine zoologists, 21

medicines, 24

oxygen, 23

parasitology, 22

parrotfish, 15, 29

photosynthesis, 23

phytoplankton, 31, 32

plankton, 15, 30, 31, 32, 38, 44

plants, 5, 6, 7, 21, 23, 37

polyps, 25

research, 4, 18, 20, 26, 27, 28–30, 32–35, 36–37, 40–41

sea cucumbers, 15

seahorses, 15

starfish, 7, 9, 11, 33–34, 40, 41

symbiosis, 19

volunteering, 16

zoologists, 21, 44

zooplankton, 31

zooxanthellae, 21

Look for More Books in This Series:

Art in Action: Have You Got What It Takes to Be an Animator?

Battling Blazes: Have You Got What It Takes to Be a Firefighter?

Cordially Invited: Have You Got What It Takes to Be an Event Planner?

Creating Cuisine: Have You Got What It Takes to Be a Chef?

Focusing on Fitness: Have You Got What It Takes to Be a Personal Trainer?

Hard Hat Area: Have You Got What It Takes to Be a Contractor?

Pop the Hood: Have You Got What It Takes to Be an Auto Technician?

Trendsetter: Have You Got What It Takes to Be a Fashion Designer?

Wild About Wildlife: Have You Got What It Takes to Be a Zookeeper?